D1379496

INSPIRATION
141 Wortley Road
London, ON   N6C 3P4
519-936-1960 *

THE WAY OUT

☆

The Way Beyond

☆

Wealth

☆

The Teacher

By The Author Of

The Impersonal Life

 DEVORSS *Publications*

The Way Out
Copyright © 1971
by Sun Publishing Co.

ISBN: 0-87516-302-5
Sixteenth Printing, 2000

DeVorss & Company, Publisher
P.O. Box 550
Marina del Rey, CA 90294-0550

For more information,
please visit our website: **www.devorss.com**

Printed in The United States of America

CONTENTS

THE WAY OUT

THE WAY OUT

WE KNOW that with many finances are often a problem. All followers of Jesus Christ should learn the law which if obeyed will enable them to rise out of all conditions of lack, limitation, inharmony, disease and unhappiness that may manifest.

You ask if this is really possible, and if there is a law which if obeyed will enable one to accomplish all that.

We say emphatically, there is such a law, and that you can be free from the fear and dominance of money, that you can have an abundance of all good things, that you can be well and happy, and can bring about an adjustment into perfect harmony of all departments of your life – if you want these things enough to train yourself to obey this law.

You say that you would do anything to obtain such wonderful blessings, if it is humanly possible.

It is not only possible, but everyone who is filled with such a desire can do it. For know a great truth, — that you are permitted to be in such unhappy conditions by your Higher Self — solely in order that you may seek and gain the knowledge, the power and the ability to control them, in order to free yourself forever from them and to assume your true place in life, and therein receive the heritage of good that is here for you, whenever you become wise and strong enough to claim it and use it for the good of others and not for selfish ends.

First know that it is all a matter of consciousness, and that you, yourself alone, are to blame for these conditions: for you alone created them and are firmly holding them in your consciousness — or they would not be so plainly manifesting. All this we are taught in those great words, *"As a man thinketh in his heart, so is he."*

We know that you have heard this stated perhaps many times before, and so often that it may have become an old story. Some of you have tried to prove it and to rid your

consciousness of all your negative thoughts;
but because it took determined and persistent
effort you soon grew tired, on account of the
·strong opposition met with, and you then
dropped back into the current of the old conditions and if anything became more helpless
than you were before.

Others may have heard of the saying, but
it did not impress them; for they could not
accept the assertion that all of the inharmonies in their lives are the result of their
own beliefs, or of their past thinking crystallized into beliefs. They preferred to blame it
all on someone else, and even God came in
for a share of the blame.

The main trouble with almost everyone is
that they do not realize how many negative
and destructive beliefs they are carrying
around with them in the subconscious realms
of mind and which creep through into the
conscious mind whenever it is free from
interest in other things.

Until you can begin to study your mind
and watch for and note these negative beliefs
when they come — and you will find that they

are actually beliefs—and refuse them further support, there is not much hope for you.

In fact it is the first thing you must learn to do. Those who are too mentally lazy to do such watching and controlling of their thoughts, are usually the ones who will not accept that their own thinking and beliefs create for them all of the conditions now manifesting in their lives.

But it makes no difference whether you accept it as being true or not—*it is the law.*

THE LAW

Now if you are ready to hear the law, we will state it in words that everyone can understand.

Note these words, and let them impress themselves on you, so that from this moment ever afterward they will live in your mind as a guiding influence.

"WHATEVER YOU THINK AND HOLD IN CONSCIOUSNESS AS BEING SO, OUT-MANIFESTS ITSELF IN YOUR BODY OR AFFAIRS."

Whether you accept this as yet or not, consider for a while the truth that every thought you think, especially those relating in any way to self, hovers around in your mental atmosphere, just as a child stays close to its parent. These thoughts being about yourself receive the life that maintains them from the *feeling* that you put into them.

In other words, the thoughts themselves are but mental forms, but when you think them with feeling of any kind you fill these forms with *life* and they become as living things which ever return to you, their parent, to be fed with more living power. For all feeling expressed is life, is vital power, and if you only knew it, all the thoughts which persistently influence your mind and harass you, are only your mental children clamoring for food and attention, and compelling more worrying, anxiety, or fear from you; all of which are excellent food containing rich vital power, and which makes them grow rapidly, until they become so powerful that in time they dominate your mind so that you can scarcely think of anything else.

When the fact is, these thoughts exist to you only *when you let them into your mind* — that is, they are of importance to you only when you give them attention and recognition. But on the other hand, their power over you and their life can quickly be nullified by simply knowing the law, and refusing to feed them longer with life power by giving them further attention or interest.

And it should not be necessary to state that *voicing* such thoughts definitely and *speedily* outmanifests them, for the spoken word is far more potent than the thought. Above all else you should guard carefully your speech, voicing nothing you do not want to see manifest. Always remember, however, that by preventing such thoughts entering the mind there will be no impulse to voice them.

So that you can see now that it *is* all a matter of consciousness, of thinking and harboring the right kind of thoughts — those you wish to outmanifest, and of letting into your mind no thoughts you do not want to manifest in your body or affairs.

And perhaps you can also see that what is ordinarily called thinking is only the admitting into your mind of thoughts that originated chiefly in other minds and which you of course attracted to you. This is also true of all negative, inharmonious and destructive thoughts — there must be something in you that attracts them or they would not come.

Many will still permit them to come, for only by the suffering, hardship and struggle to escape from their influence that you undergo, will you learn how to free yourself and gain the power to control and consciously direct your life to constructive ends.

That is the *hard* way, but we are now going to show you the *true* way to free yourself forever from fear and worry about finances, and from all other destructive forces.

We are assuming that all who read are students and followers of Christ's teachings. You remember those significant words of His in the Sermon on the Mount.

*"Take no thought (or be not anxious) say-
ing, what shall we eat, or what shall we drink,
or wherewithal shall we be clothed;*

*"For your heavenly Father knoweth that
ye have need of all these things.*

*"But seek ye first the Kingdom (Conscious-
ness) of God, and His righteousness (Right
Ideas); and all these things will be added
unto you."*

We know that these words seem important
to you, but we also know that very few take
them as actual promises and try definitely
and determinedly to put them to the proof.

But that is the very thing you *must* do, if
you would obey the law; and when we show
you how to free yourself from fear and worry
you will not only be able to free yourself
from the power money has over you, but you
will have found the straight and narrow way
to the Kingdom. And all the powers of the
Kingdom will help you, if you are strong and
determined enough to win the goal. For the

Kingdom of God and His righteousness is only a *state of consciousness where we do right thinking* — where we think God's thoughts only.

Can you do that? Surely you can — if you *will.* Then this is the way:

THE WAY

You must train yourself to STAND GUARD CONTINUALLY AT THE DOOR OF YOUR MIND, AND TO LET IN NO THOUGHTS OR FEELINGS THAT YOU DO NOT WANT TO OUTMANIFEST.

Think this over carefully, and you will see that it is the only way.

It may seem hard — at first, and you may not know what to admit and what to deny. But guard the door from every *negative* thought and feeling of whatsoever nature — from every thought that you know God would not have you think; from every doubt, fear, worry, anxiety, or concern of any kind; from every tendency to criticize, judge or

condemn anybody or anything or any condition; from self-pity, jealousy, envy, irritation,
unkindness, anger, hatred, etc. These will give
you an idea of what are negative and ungod-
like thoughts, and which must no longer have
a part in your consciousness.

If you will keep all such untrue thoughts
out of your mind, you can see that then and
then only can your Higher Self draw into
your mind the true and positive thoughts that
will attract to you the good that is waiting
to manifest itself to you. For while your
mind is cluttered with all those fearful, worrying, discouraged, sick, weak, poverty-tainted
thoughts, how can you expect anyone who
feels these vibrations—and vibrations are
things you cannot cover up—to be attracted
to you, or how can you expect God to inspire
you with thoughts of a beneficial nature?

In fact, such negative thoughts actually
keep away the things you are longing to have
manifest in your life—for like attracts like.
Think! Poverty-stricken thoughts do not
attract prosperity or jobs; sick thoughts do
not build a healthy consciousness; and belief

that you are a failure invites failure.

You say this all sounds good, but when one is sunk so deep in conditions that no matter which way he turns he sees only sickness, hunger, poverty or failure facing him, despite months of effort to conquer the condition, to get work, or to do something to tide over till better days come, — how is he to think of anything else?

Yes, dear friend, we see what you are up against, but we also see that you are caught fast between the horns of a dilemma. You have sought help from the world of men and it has turned you down. You have exhausted all the forces of self, and you admit that you are completely helpless. And perhaps you have even prayed to God, and seemingly He has not heard, or He has not answered you.

But where — *who* is this God to whom you have prayed? Is he somewhere up in the skies, or in some hazy place, you know not where?

Have you prayed to God *within* you? Have you turned there and opened your heart to *Him,* deep within your self, in the Kingdom, where your Higher Self abides?

If not, dear friend, then after reading this article carefully until you truly get its full meaning for you, pray to Him *there;* get down on your knees and in deep and true humility pour out your heart to Him, knowing that He *as your Higher Self* hears you, that He does know that you have need of all these things, and that He *will* answer you.

Go back to those words in the Sermon on the Mount and read them over again and again, until you get all of their wondrous meaning and realize that they are meant *for you,* and that they are a definite promise made by the Master *to you—that if you will do what you are there told to do,* the Father will give to you all things that you need.

Think! This is Jesus' promise to you, and therefore it *will* be fulfilled—*if you do your part.*

YOU CAN DO IT

You *can* do it, you *must* do it—if you would have the blessings which He promises you, and which we promise you when we say that you can have an abundance of all good things and that you can be free from the dominance of money forever.

And what must you do? You must not be anxious or worry anymore about what you shall eat or drink or what you shall wear, for your loving Father knows that you must have all of these things. But if you will seek first His Kingdom—that is, His Consciousness, where you must think only His thoughts for you—as we have shown you how to do, and then will do what He tells you to do when His thoughts come into your mind, He will provide you with all the good things He has had in store for you from the beginning.

We know that we are telling you to do what now seems almost impossible. But, dear friend, this is *the only way* to win these blessings; and you say you will do anything to obtain them, if it is humanly possible.

It is not only possible, but it is the very thing ordained and intended for you by your Higher Self—or He would not have brought this message to you and placed this ultimatum so squarely before you.

You have tried your way, and you have tried the world's way, and you know where they have brought you. And now you are given the opportunity of trying God's way! The way laid out for you in the beginning. Can you not see that it is now the *only* way for you?

Thus God brings His children that love Him finally to realize that they cannot serve both God and Mammon. For they must be shown that they are serving Mammon just as much by fearing him and yielding to the power of money, as they would be by openly worshipping money and becoming its slave when having great quantities of it. They must be made to see that by fearing money's seeming power they are making it first and God second in their lives, and until they truly want to serve God more than any other thing, and *prove* it by their *right thinking, speech and actions*, they are not yet where His help can reach them.

THE ULTIMATUM

So this is the ultimatum that you are facing.

You have now come to the place where God
holds out His hand to you, and says:

"My child, I would help you. But it means
that you must give yourself and all your ideas
over wholly to Me, must learn to think only
My thoughts, speak only what I would say,
and do only what I would have you to do. It
means that you must *not* let into your mind
or believe any other thoughts, no matter what
appearances are or how much such thoughts
beg for admittance.

"You have had *your* chance and you see
what a sorry mess you have made of things.
Now if you are willing utterly and completely
to trust *Me,* and to wait upon and serve Me
only, and will keep your mind and heart clean
and empty of all untrue thoughts so that I
may fill them with My thoughts, I will inspire
in you the ideas that will lift you quickly out
of your present consciousness—which means
out of present conditions—into one where
peace, harmony and plenty will be your
mental children, that will ever come to
you to be fed with loving *trust* in Me, *con-*

fidence in your power to express Me, and with the pure *joy* of living, that you will then be feeling as the natural and continuous state of your consciousness."

Is this worth trying for? Do you really want it?

Then what are you going to do about it?

If you are willing to make a supreme effort and to put all the power of your will into it; will make yourself a *positive* agent of your Father's Will, looking only and always to Him to guide and inspire you, you will truly receive all the help you need, and will find, if you persist despite any discouragements that may come testing your determination, that you will then walk straight into the good that has long been waiting for you.

APPEARANCES

This means that from this moment you must pay no more attention to appearances, for what is now appearing is but the outmanifestation of what you formerly visualized in your thinking, and which your fearing and worrying crystallized into facts and fastened upon you.

Try to realize the great significance of this. It is not what you *see* as conditions surrounding you that really counts—it is what you *believe* is so. And when you *know*—as we have proven to you—that *what you believe* is the cause of what is manifesting outwardly *as it now appears,* you will definitely begin to change your beliefs into those you *want* to manifest.

Think this over, for it is the only way you can change conditions and their appearances, —you must remove from your consciousness the beliefs you are holding there, by replacing them with beliefs you want to see manifest in your life and affairs.

How can you do this—when you cannot help but believe the things that stare you in the face, no matter which way you turn?

THE WAY OUT

We will now show you the way, a way so

simple and easy that anyone can do it, if they will obey exactly what we tell them to do.

All that is needed is to say over and over again to yourself *until you believe it absolutely,* letting not a single doubt of its truth ever enter your mind, the following words:

"GOD LOVES AND CARES FOR ME AND IS GIVING ME ALL GOOD THINGS.

"I LOVE HIM AND THINK HIS THOUGHTS AND DO ONLY THE THINGS HE WANTS ME TO DO."

Try to realize the full truth of these words, to *feel* it, to *see* yourself actually living in the consciousness of it, going about your daily work in that consciousness. If you *do* this, it will bring the greatest possible blessings into your life.

The first statement should not be hard to believe, for you surely know that He loves and cares for you; for whether you know it yet or not, everything that has come into your life has been good for you, for through these things He has brought you to the place where you should be willing to look to and trust Him only, so that His love and care *can* give you all the good things He has had for you from the beginning.

And it should be easy to love Him, and through consciously loving and trying to think His thoughts, you can see that it opens your mind so that His thoughts come into it, and can thus direct you just what to do that will bring success, prosperity, health, harmony and happiness into your life.

Dear friends, we wish that we could reveal the truth of the above wonderful statements so clearly to you that they will *live* with you and will motivate your every thought, word and act forever afterward. They are so mighty in their truth that if lived *they will make you more than man.*

So do not pass them by because they seem so simple and commonplace. Stay with them until all their glorious import dawns upon you and you feel the change that they will surely and quickly bring into your consciousness and therefore into your life and all your affairs.

DEFINITE INSTRUCTIONS

And now for instructions of a concrete nature. Let us take some definite good that you want to have manifest in your life – we do not mean *things,* but conditions that will bring harmony and happiness to yourself and dear ones; which means that you must *make sure that it is good, that it is what the God of you wants you to have.* That should be easy, for He has ordained all good things for you – but you must *know* that and be able to *see* it as good.

Then build in your mind a picture of that good. Build it perfect, in every detail, so that it stands out clear and distinct *as a finished and accomplished fact.* According to how complete and distinct is this picture in your mind is it actually finished on the mental plane – the plane of concrete mental forms, which determines its physical appearance –

and is it ready to come forth into manifestation.

And now if you will follow exactly the same process which brought into manifestation all of the present unwanted conditions in your life, only using the opposite kind of thoughts and feelings, as we shall indicate, you can bring forth into perfect manifestation this picture now existing on the mental plane and awaiting the action of your will.

We will take as an illustration a friend who recently lost her position. Several weeks before, this friend mentioned to the writer that their business was very poor and that they had laid off several who had charge of departments similar to hers, and she supposed she would be the next to go. The writer remonstrated with her and tried to show that that attitude of mind would bring to her what she did not want. Two weeks later another friend reported that she had said the same thing to her, and we do not know to how many others she had voiced it. But a few days afterward, as she had pictured it, the notice of her dismissal came.

Now let us analyze the mental process which created and brought to pass the losing of her position.

The conditions of the business, the letting go of other department heads and clerks naturally caused our friend to build a picture in her mind of her also probably having to go sooner or later, and through the *fear* of it she actually *saw* herself leaving. Day after day the conditions in the office, her talks with fellow employees and with others in other businesses in similar bad straits, and with those who had lost their jobs, increased and intensified her fear and helped her to build in the details of her picture, until she had it all finished and perfect. Then she naturally *felt* she would soon have to go. So of course it *had* to come to pass.

Now do you understand? The proof that she and she alone created the necessity of her going was, (1) she was the last of all the heads of departments let go, for she was the most efficient; (2) she began criticizing her employers and their actions; (3) she learned afterward that they did not want to lose her and they might give her back her position, having hired two young men to replace the other women let go.

But she had created on the mental plane the finished thought form of being dismissed and had vitalized it with her fears and other feelings, and as a result that thought form had to outmanifest; and so it forced itself into the minds of her employers and impelled them to do what they otherwise would not have done.

Now let us apply similar thought processes to the bringing forth of the good you pictured above into manifestation.

You have built and now see the finished picture of that good, but now instead of seeing a negative outmanifestation of that picture, we will see a positive and happy one. So every day and as often as possible during the day you will see your pictured good manifesting, affecting your life in every way you can visualize it; see yourself actually enjoying it and sharing it with your dear ones and friends; and all the time you are seeing it consciously pouring deep feelings of joy, of

love and gratitude into your sense of its being
an actual and living reality, your own creation,
the product of your own spirit, which you
are nursing and bringing forth into physical
being.

And just as surely as our friend brought
forth her unwanted creation into actuality, so
must your good come forth and be to you all
that you visioned and intended it to be. It is
the law, and a faithful following of this
process in all constructive thinking and
creating will always bring the results sought,
even as your destructive thinking brought the
results unsought.

Study the above examples and explanation
until the process stands out clear and true to
you. Then study your own individual case
until you see plainly how you came to your
present state. Then begin to reverse your
thought processes as shown above, until you
express along constructive lines only.

Your sincere desire to free yourself—not
just to ease yourself from suffering and hardship, but to *know the truth*, to learn the cause
of being in any unwanted condition, and to

gain the ability to free yourself from it, so you can help others to get free — will draw to you the help needed, and you will in time be free. Do not give up if your mind does not respond immediately, for it has formed the habit of wrong seeing and thinking, and you were a long time forming present conditions. Just know that if you persist until your mind sees that you are determined and really mean it, it will soon fall in line and follow the new ways of thinking you lay down for it as easily as it did the old ways in the past.

The main thing is to remember always that you are dealing and working with mental substance on the mental plane, and are not concerned with outer appearances and conditions, for you know that by such work you are shaping and changing conditions to those you wish to be manifest.

WE HAVE now shown you the Law. We have explained to you its operation. We have made clear that by wrong thinking and believing you have brought upon yourself the conditions now surrounding you, and we have shown you how to free yourself from these conditions and how to create those you wish to manifest in your life. There now remain only a few more things to tell you to help impress it all upon your mind so that it will become a part of your consciousness.

BE POSITIVE

The first is the importance of always being *positive* in your thinking, *positive* in your speaking, and *positive* in your doing. *And never negative.*

The negative person attracts all the negative things of life, all the ills, inharmonies, troubles that are in the mental atmosphere – the effluvia of other weak and negative minds; while a positive person attracts all the good. If you understand the radio you will know that when you set your dial at a certain wave length, all that is "on the air" of that wave length will make itself heard. It is exactly the same with your mind; it will receive whatever happens to be "on the air" of the wave length to which your thoughts are attuned. So that it is "up to you" and you only what your mind radio gives forth or outmanifests.

Have you ever noticed how a positive person in a crowd of ordinary persons is always the center of attraction, always makes his or her presence felt, and always accomplishes things that lesser ones never think of? A most forcible illustration was once when driving on a thoroughfare where there was a temporary narrow road built at the side of where a new bridge was being constructed, we came to a halt because of a long line of automobiles ahead. After waiting for some minutes the writer got out and noticed perhaps thirty cars on the long decline to the bottom of the ravine and a similar line up the hill on the other side. But seemingly the left side of the road was clear all through. He could not see any sense in waiting, so he pulled out and started ahead and went through without opposition. While going up the other side he looked back and found a great string of cars following him, and a man in one of these told

him that they had been waiting back there
for twenty minutes. Evidently two cars from
opposite directions had come together with
others following them, and they were afraid
they could not get through on the narrow
road, because of other cars coming.

It is always so in life; the positive soul gets
there, the negative one stays behind, or tags
along when he finds a leader. Why be negative? It is all an attitude of mind, and can be
changed simply by changing your beliefs.

Besides we are all sons and daughters of
God, children of the greatest King in the
world. Who naturally gives all the riches and
good things of His Kingdom to all those of us
who know it is our divine heritage and who
will accept and enjoy them.

A KING'S SON

Try to realize that you are the equal — nay
the superior — of any world Prince, the son of
the King of any World Kingdom; for our
Father's Kingdom includes his father's kingdom; and if we could lift our minds to the

consciousness of our true Selves as sons of
God, we would go about KNOWING that all
that our Father, the King, has is ours, and
that all of the Father's servants will rush to
supply — to anticipate — our every need. This is
actually so. Each one can experience it. All
you need is to *believe* it, and to go about in
that consciousness, even as does the Prince of
any world kingdom in his lesser kingdom
consciousness.

Then as a King's son you must learn, if all
that your Father has is yours, to spend freely
of the riches He has given you with absolute
fearlessness. For there is no limit to them,
no lack of wealth, for it is always available —
His resources are inexhaustible.

You must acquire this consciousness, you
must feel even as does the other Prince about
spending or using money Think you that he
has any fear of lack or limitation of supply?
No, there is always a great plenty for his
every need, for his every comfort, every
pleasure, for every constructive idea; for he
knows that back of him is his father, the
King, and all the resources of his kingdom. So

must you learn to know that back of you is your Father-God, with all the resources of His Kingdom.

USE MONEY FEARLESSLY

The quickest way to rid your mind of that old fear of want, fear of your job, fear of the power of money, is to have an absolute trust in your heavenly Father's loving care and for you *to pay out gladly your last dollar for a needed thing,* KNOWING that by so doing you make it possible for Him to supply you *with plenty more.*

It is as if your needs must keep the stream of money ever flowing, if you would not clog up its source. For money, in its true sense, is the means for the perfect expression of material life; even as the blood is the means for the perfect expression of physical health.

In both cases your mind must not only hold true and pure thoughts—God's thoughts only—about the material life of yourself and others, and about your physical well-being, but you must know that God's Mind is the

Source of all true thoughts; and by perfect faith and trust in Him you thus keep yourself open to the free circulation of His Thoughts in your consciousness about both your affairs and your body, thus creating perfect health and harmony in both.

This has been proven by many so-called "tithers." They have created a consciousness where they know that, by using money freely in such perfect trust in God, and especially in thanksgiving and loving gratitude to Him, giving freely a percentage of their income to that part of His Work which is bringing the Truth to them, they become greatly blessed in this world's goods and are put in a position where they can help many souls to come into this same truth.

It is the pinching and holding on to your last dollar, fearing that no more will come, that actually prevents your receiving more. For giving, more than anything else, helps to open the channel so that supply, both spiritual and material, can freely flow.

Now we wish finally to emphasize that the application and proving of this great law not only will bring financial freedom and success, but it will bring also perfect health, harmony, and happiness into all departments of your life. For when you begin to think only true thoughts about yourself, then of course God's consciousness lives in your body and His thoughts rule your mind, and there can manifest only perfect health in your body and perfect harmony in all your various affairs; when naturally happiness *must* sing in your heart and be your daily companion.

So, dear friend, we have given you this message — one born of an intense yearning to furnish to those who are wandering in the darkness of present world conditions a sure guide to lead them back into the Light of Love, of abiding Trust, and of true Happiness.

———————

If the Message, THE WAY OUT, strongly impressed you and especially if it was the means of freeing you from desperate conditions from which there seemed no way out, we earnestly urge that you do all you can to get it in the hands of those of your friends who need its saving help.

THE WAY BEYOND

THE WAY BEYOND

IN OUR booklet, "THE WAY OUT," was pointed the way to freedom from lack, limitation, inharmony, disease and unhappiness, and there is no excuse for any who faithfully follow the suggestions given to be any longer in such condition.

The booklet has reached scores of thousands of readers and many have been lifted by its truths into a new consciousness and thereby into a new world, where everything and everybody are changed, for they are seeing with new eyes and with a different understanding. That which appears is no longer what it seemed, but the good and the real are now visible and can be seen shining through all conditions and people—*because they are now looked for*, and the former negative tendencies are tabooed and not allowed to enter the consciousness.

This is not the case with all of course, for a great number have not been able to conquer those tendencies which so long have been permitted to rule. The press of circumstances and the negative conditions everywhere manifest seemingly have been too much for them and they have become utterly discouraged, not knowing that they actually have within themselves the power to rise out of these conditions, and that help is waiting the moment they awaken from their despondency and definitely determine to do the best they can to prove the truth of what was stated in the booklet.

It is for such that this new Message is written, with the earnest desire that all who read will be so inspired by its truths that they will make the necessary effort and will thus receive the good that has been waiting for them from the beginning.

We first urge that everyone who reads procure a copy of "THE WAY OUT," if one is not already owned, and that it be studied carefully and prayerfully. It will do good merely to read it, or even to study it, unless what is given you to do *is faithfully TRIED until proven* — that is, tried day after day *in all your thinking, speaking and acting,* for at least one month. If you will do it that long, we promise that such a change will manifest in your consciousness — and likewise in your affairs — that it will be a turning point in your life, and you will never again return to the old way of thinking and acting.

Is it not then worth the effort? Then do not let anything prevent your making a supreme effort, asking God to give you the strength and ability to accomplish what we have shown.

GOD WITHIN YOU

Now, we are going to try to make clear to you the statement in "THE WAY OUT," that God is *within you;* make it so clear that never more will you think of Him as somewhere up in the skies, nor will you be uncertain as to who or what He is.

First try to realize that the life animating and growing you is not your life, that you have no control over it, that it does things to you, causes you to do things, puts you through all the experiences you are undergoing without your consent, and that seemingly it knows just what it is doing and must have a very wise and loving purpose in doing it.

Likewise the consciousness that you call yours seemingly receives all its ideas, thoughts and impressions wholly independently of your will or desire. They come into your mind when they will, influence your feelings and actions continually, and you have little power to prevent it. Also you will admit that you have no power of your own, that you can think, speak and do only as the power to do these things is given you *from within.*

And that Something doing all this, unquestionably is a greater, far wiser and a very loving Something that knows always what to do, knows the end before the beginning, and is apparently trying to teach your human mind about Itself, teach it the lessons contained in each experience, and the laws back of life and of physical manifestation.

Because that Something is so different from

and yet is so intimate a part of what you call
you, It must be akin to what is termed God.
We have called It the Higher Self, and it is in
fact very *God in you.* It is like a ray or reflection of God's mind shining somewhere deep
within your consciousness—a "light which
shineth in the darkness, but the darkness (of
the outer human mind) knoweth it not." For
certainly when It can get your mind's attention and you listen, It displays a wisdom that
is as near to that God as the human mind can
conceive. And those who heed and obey are
given a glimpse of something wonderful,
which while inexpressible is altogether divine
and most satisfying.

GOD IS ALL IN ALL

You have heard the statement that God is
All in All, and of "the light which lighteth
every man that cometh into the world." Then
that light *must* be a ray of God's Mind that
shines in the darkness of the human mind,
ever trying to make it aware of its Divine
Source *within itself*—the Mind of God, from

which it derives all that it is, all that it has,
and all power to be, to know or to do anything.

Then think, if God is All in All, He is in
everything and *in everybody* – no matter what
it is or who he is. It must be so! Yet who of
us always sees and acknowledges Him *in* such?

And because we do not acknowledge Him
in His manifestations, refuse to see Him, and
call Him everything He is *not*, we see instead
all the error, the evil and the lies that our
darkened minds have accepted as real, lose
ourselves in the maze of our "separate" misconceptions; and in consequence endure the
inharmonies, disease and suffering of minds
thinking themselves apart from the Consciousness that includes them and all that is.

God being All in All, then all things and
all men are good and perfect. They could not
be otherwise, when God and His goodness and
perfection are everywhere.

But make no mistake, when stating that all
things and all men are good and perfect, we
are not speaking of what you with your "separate" mind and present understanding see

and believe; we are not speaking of "appearances"—of your separate mind's creations. For what you see now are only the pictures you have built in your mind of what you *thought* was the truth—before you really *knew* about God's being All in All and ever showing forth His goodness, beauty and perfection in everything—to those who have eyes to see.

Therefore it is necessary first to convince your mind of the truth, so that it can be free itself of all these untrue beliefs—these false pictures of God and of His expressions of Himself that it has built and is carrying around in its consciousness.

Then listen! God, Who is All in All and Who is all good and all perfect, must be also all wise, all loving and all powerful. Anything less than these is not of God, but must be man's wrong, ignorant, and distorted concepts of God and of His expressions of Himself. Think that out until you see how true it is.

Then all things of an inharmonious or unhappy nature that you see, whatever they be that are less than good or perfect, are only what *you think* is so, because of ignorance or wrong teaching. And so long as you continue to believe these things are real, they will continue to be real to you, no matter what they are, whether they pertain to the conditions surrounding you, to your body, to your self, to your affairs, or to those invisible things which relate to and affect your life, health and happiness.

GOD IS THE REAL YOU

Now let us relate this truth of God being All in All to yourself. If He is all we have stated, then He must be the *real you,* must be that higher, greater you we pointed out earlier in this message, whose life is animating your body, whose mind is influencing all your thoughts, speech and actions, and whose power enables you to do all things that you do. It must then be His Consciousness that is your consciousness, but stepped down through your Higher Self to your soul and then to your human mind, expressing Itself on the Spiritual plane in your Higher Self as the Christ Consciousness, on the soul plane in your soul or soul consciousness, and on the physical plane in your brain mind as mortal consciousness. But it is all God's Consciousness relayed down through your Higher Self, and enabling you to be as much aware of God, the Real Self of you and the One Self of all men (for is He not All in All?) as the channel of your darkened mortal mind has been illumined to perceive Him and to partake of His Consciousness.

It is said that to Know God, man must first know his self. And when you truly know that you are not a thing of flesh and blood, but are a human soul or a center of consciousness, clothed by a garment of flesh, even as your soul clothes your Real or Christ Self—the Holy Spirit or Consciousness of God—as we have shown above, you can begin to understand how God actually is within you—IS you.

Now let us consider you first as a soul, a center of consciousness, and then we will try to show you the relation of your soul to your human mind and your Higher, Spiritual Self.

You in your integrity are a soul and are pure consciousness. In other words you are that which is conscious or aware of all that comes to you from without through the avenue of your five senses, or through vibrations which they are not sensitive enough to perceive, such as impressions or thoughts from other centers of consciousness. All of these sensations are brought to your consciousness through the mediumship of your human mind, while the vibrations mentioned are received directly by the soul and are interpreted to the mind according to how the mind has been prepared to understand them.

As a soul or consciousness you are distinct from your human mind, for the mind serves merely as an instrument to receive and inform you of what comes from without in the world of matter. Yet your mind is in reality an outer extension of your soul consciousness, slowed down to the mental capacity of your human brain, there serving as your agent in the informing you of all things going on in the physical world and the carrying out of your instructions pertaining to that world.

In that partial and necessarily limited consciousness, your mind grew to think itself a self and separate from you in your soul consciousness. In this fancied separateness it gradually filled its consciousness with all those wrong concepts and beliefs about physical and mental things spoken of above, which grew so real and tangible in its consciousness that they in time ruled all your thoughts, speech and actions. And this outer and fancied separate consciousness is what constitutes your lower or mortal self.

But these concepts and beliefs should have no influence over your soul consciousness — only as you let them. The proof is, when you get quiet and still your mind and shut out all thoughts and impressions coming from without, then you are in your pure soul consciousness and are free to be aware of the impressions coming from *within* your soul. For then you learn that deep within the soul there is a higher consciousness and a Spiritual intelligence that presses the soul from within informing you of *Spiritual* things, even as the outer mind's consciousness presses from

without to inform you of material things.
And that higher or innermost consciousness
is that of your Higher or Divine Self.

In reality there is only one Self, but this
enables you to see how the Higher Self, the
Spirit of God in man, reaches down or out
from the center of man's being in Divine Consciousness into the soul consciousness, and
thence outward into the mortal mind, giving
to man's brain its consciousness, which causes
man to think his consciousness separate, when
it is only the consciousness of God thinned
down to the brain mind's capacity to hold
and use it.

YOUR GOD SELF

Then the Higher Self, this Spirit of God
deep within you, is the real you, is the Self
that has ever been directing all the activities
of your life, has been actually doing all
through you, knows just what He is doing,
assumes all responsibility and evidently sees
the end before the beginning.

Then you can realize that of your human self you do nothing, and never did anything; that all the power, knowledge and life you have comes from your Higher Self; and that if you ever wish to be, to do, or to have anything, and to gain the freedom, happiness and peace your soul seeks, it behooves you to get well acquainted with that Self, to learn to cooperate with Him, and to wait upon and serve Him in all the activities of your life.

From this you can also realize that the reason you failed to gain any of these things in the past, is because you tried to get them without reckoning upon your Higher Self or knowing His part in the doing—you tried to do it alone. So He let you fail again and again, until you came to that place where you learned the uselessness of trying to do anything yourself, and you became willing to turn to Him and humbly ask Him to take charge and you gladly yielded over all to Him and put all your trust in Him.

Everyone must come to that place—every seeker of the true way of life; for until self with its human mind has been completely

humbled and gives up utterly, it cannot accept
the truth of its non-reality and of the actuality
of the God-man within, and that *He* can do all
and will provide all things—when the human
mind yields itself wholly to Him.

If you who read have come to that place,
and are truly ready to give yourself to the
God Self within, then we will tell you of a
great but simple law that you must follow.

A SIMPLE LAW

That Law is—*"Whatever is before you to
do, do it the best you know how, in order to
please your God-Self."* For He placed you just
where you now are and provided the particular
task confronting you as the best means and
opportunity in which to teach your human
mind the next lessons you are to learn, and to
develop in you the spiritual qualities you still
lack in order to make your human self a
perfect instrument for His use.

Then in doing that task, for He provides all
tasks and brings you to all problems, having

now given yourself over wholly to Him, you
are concerned only that you do what is before
you the best you can, KNOWING that He will
provide the power, understanding and ability
needed, and that you are not responsible any
more for results, as they are all in His keep-
ing. For have you not put the full responsibility on Him, are now trusting everything to
Him, and consequently you no longer have
any fears, doubts or worries to clog your
mind and prevent His accomplishing His
purpose for you? Only by thus yielding all to
Him can you be a clean and open channel
through which He can bring through into
being the good and perfect things He intends
to manifest in your life. For He can intend
nothing less than that, else why all the trouble
He is taking with you?

It is all a matter of trusting, dear friend,
of trusting the God within you. If you have
failed in the past, no matter how hard you
tried, it is because *you did not trust enough.*

Therefore we are bringing this great truth
closer by asking you *truly* to trust the God
within, your Higher Self, *the Christ* of you,

Who we have shown has all the wisdom and
power of God; to let go utterly and *put ALL
your trust in Him.*

You must learn thus to trust, until it
becomes the supreme and dominant influence
in your consciousness, for

THE ONLY THING THAT PREVENTS
YOUR GOOD FROM COMING INTO NAT-
URAL AND CONTINUOUS EXPRESSION
IS YOUR LACK OF REAL FAITH AND
TRUST IN THE GOD WITHIN YOU —
YOUR CHRIST SELF.

This means that if instead of faith and trust
you still let fears, doubts and worries into
your mind, then of course there they cause
you to build negative pictures of the things
you are fearing, and you proceed to entertain
and feed them by further fears, until they
become actual living things in your mental
world. In time they largely control your
mind and you are helpless. And naturally
every time you succumb to them, you
grow more helpless.

Is this not true? – Then what is the solution? Only one thing. You must let go completely and turn the whole problem over to God. Do that actually – "wash your hands" of it, "step out from under," and throw the entire responsibility upon Him.

Think! Can you do that? *Try* it. In fact, He wants you to do it. Talk to this God within the Real Self of you, and tell Him that *you are through*, that you have done your best, and that is all you *can do* – and it was useless. And now *it is up to Him;* He will have to handle it. *Actually mean it,* and then *let go* – and truly "wash your hands" of all responsibility.

Then, and not until then, has He got your mind in the state where it is ready to hear His Voice and learn what He has in store for you. For once it has really thrown off the burden of self, there is no longer a negative force attracting the old fears, doubts and worries. Instead you become a positive force in your believing that He now will take care of all things, for you intend to do nothing and to give Him the chance to prove what *He* can do.

AN ABSOLUTE LETTING GO

It is to just that state of mind He desires to bring you, where you actually let go, giving the load you are carrying over to Him, and thereby become as free as a little child, just such a child as we will now picture to you.

Standing on the sidewalk of a busy street waiting for the light signal, is a little boy of three years whose hand is tightly clasped in that of his father. Then they start across. Is the child frightened by the big automobiles and the noise and tumult at this busy corner? No, he sees and knows no danger and gleefully enjoys the turmoil and the mixing with the crowd hurrying across—for he *knows* that Dad is taking care of him and will not let any harm come to him. Just as he unconsciously knows that Dad will feed and clothe him, for to him Dad is as God who will provide everything he needs and take every care of him.

Think you your God-Self does not love you and is not taking equal care of you, His child? For are you not a part of His Being and does He not need you to express His Self?

Then how could He let you really suffer or come to any harm? What your human mind suffers and the dangers it fears are only the nightmares of childhood which disappear when the light of understanding is brought. Besides such mental suffering actually burns away the qualities of self that hinder His perfect expression, while through the fears that come and persist He teaches you how to become strong.

It is these mental fears—for they are purely mental, that is, they exist in your mind, *not in His Consciousness*—that are clogging your mind-channel, and preventing His pouring through it the good that awaits.

Then you will have to cleanse your mind of all such negative things—of every doubt, fear or worry, and especially of those *wrong pictures* you are carrying around in your consciousness. Do you still *see* yourself as sick, or ailing, or poor, or very much needing anything? Then can you not realize it is that picture which is clogging up the channel? For what you think and carry around in consciousness as being so always outmanifests itself. How can the good you wish to manifest get by that picture?

That is the whole trouble, dear friend,—you have not cleansed your mind of those old picture-beliefs, some of which are hiding down in the dark corners of your subconsciousness, purposely refusing to come out into the light; for they know, the moment you see them for what they are, their days are numbered. In fact, you must go down into the subconsciousness and dig out all of such and cast them forth; for until the whole mind is clean and free of all negative and untrue thoughts and feelings and *is kept so,* it cannot be brought into your God Consciousness where there are only positive, true, good and perfect ideas about you and you can see all things in their reality, even as He sees, and you can know as He knows; your mind thus becoming a perfect channel through which He can give you your divine heritage which He has so long had waiting for you.

IMAGINE THE GOD-YOU

Now we ask you to try to imagine yourself in the Consciousness of your God-Self and to see with His eyes this self you call you, and the other selves around you and the world you live in.

In the first place, know that as He is all wise, all loving and all powerful, and is still you, but a perfect you, He must have a perfect mind and body — but not like your physical self. His body is that "image and likeness of God" in which man was originally formed. And if God made man like Himself, who could change man — a perfect being? Not even man, himself.

Then man must still be perfect! Yes, it cannot be otherwise. For think you anyone could alter or bring to naught any perfect thing God created?

We know you are asking how then did man become so changed. He is *not* changed — the *real* man. He is your Higher Self — the *Real* You — the perfect Man, just as God created him, as He now sees him, and as he will always be.

Now listen! What you and others see are *mortal man's* creations—not God's. They are merely the creations of man's fancied "separate" mind, and have no existence except in his brain-mind's consciousness. When God gave man free-will, He gave him the power *to think* as he wills, which means *to create.* He could think good—God's thoughts, or evil—not God's thoughts. Man did not realize his God nature then; he had only his human nature to judge by, and the only way to learn was, not by taking God's or anyone's word for things, but by thinking, by trying and finding what his creations—the things, conditions and people of his world—*were not.* And so he thought and created and tried from the beginning to make perfect things and conditions in this world of his consciousness— with the results you see everywhere about you.

Not that many men back through the ages have not learned the truth—the truth we are trying to teach you,—that they can do nothing of themselves, but with the help of the God within them they can do all things,

can have all things, can be all things. And with
His help such have come into and are now
dwelling in their Christ Consciousness, are
One with Him, and are doing the Father s
Work on earth even as others are doing it in
Heaven.

THE CHRIST CONSCIOUSNESS

And what do they see in this Consciousness? They see that they are souls, living in a
perfect world, where every soul is young,
good, beautiful and perfect, even as the
Father conceived them, and where everything
is devised for the free use and enjoyment of
its inhabitants. Which means that there is a
rich abundance of all good things for everyone always available. No one there ever needs
anything, for it is always at hand. There any
desired thing is created by thought and you
can have it when and as you wish it. Then of
course no one takes from another or owes
another anything, for everyone has everything
he wants; because all he has to do is to see
clearly in his mind what he wants and it takes

shape and substance right before his eyes,
ready and perfect for his use.

From this you can see there is no selfishness there, for all there are those in whom self
no longer is. There is no injustice, for the law
of justice rules everyone's consciousness.
There is no evil, for it has been learned that
evil, sin, sickness, inharmony, and unhappiness are the creations of mortal mind, and of
course one who is selfless is in his Christ
Consciousness and no longer thinks and
thereby creates such things.

Does this help you to see how and why
man is responsible for this outer world – that
it is his own creation, and not God's creation?
And can you now see what is God's world –
His Kingdom, your heavenly home, where
you can return as a Prodigal Son anytime you
will be remembering and seeing only the
truth, and where you will find your heavenly
Father waiting for you with outstretched
arms?

And Who is this heavenly Father? He is
your own Real Self, the God-You, that is
always back in that Consciousness deep within

your soul, where you can retire any moment
you will. All you have to do is to throw off
everything that presses upon your consciousness from the outer world of the human mind
and turn your attention to the inner world of
Spirit. Especially must you refuse to see, to
talk about, or let your mind dwell upon
outer conditions, no matter how hard they
appear or how they seemingly affect you;
for remember they exist only in the world
of man's mind, and not in the real world
the God-You sees and lives in. If you resolutely do this, it will not be long before you
will have evidence of the reality of this
Kingdom within, and you will hear His Voice
and receive definite guidance as to what He
wills and what is His purpose for you. For
He must have a purpose, or why all this
disciplining and developing of your mind
and character? Make no mistake, He knows
what He is doing and why; and when you
have given self entirely over to Him, He will
take you into His Consciousness, and there
you will work with Him to accomplish what
He intended from the beginning.

The beautiful part of it is that there are others there working with you, others who have found Him within themselves, have found there a new and wonderful self, a wonderful world, and wonderful comrades in it; a world far more real than the ever-changing one of their own creation.

Yes, they have found their eternal home, the Kingdom of God's Consciousness, the same home which Jesus described in His many parables, when trying to tell of it to the people of His day, where He went after His mission was accomplished; where He now lives and works among His disciples who have followed Him there. To them He is a very real and actual Teacher, Guide and Friend, Who is preparing them for the great day when He will make Himself manifest to all His followers on earth and will bring Heaven down to earth to be truly in the midst of men.

THE NEXT STEP

This shows you what is possible to him who learns to think only true thoughts about himself and about all in his world. Some wonderful truths have been unfolded to you, and now it surely will be easier for you to do the things you have found you must do, if you would free yourself from the old consciousness and the conditions surrounding you and would enter the new consciousness awaiting.

The way out has been shown you. But *you* must walk in it, no one can do that for you. You cannot be shoved, nor can you jump or slide into the Kingdom — you have to earn your right to enter, have to walk every step of the way there, no matter how difficult and steep grows the path. It is no journey to be taken by the half-hearted and weak-kneed.

If you are now convinced of the truth of what was shown, the next step then is to *try to prove its truth,* first by getting thoroughly acquainted with this Real Self of you, by seeing Him as yourself, and by going about in His Consciousness. Practice this daily until you actually feel Him within, feel Him giving you of His power, of His vitalizing life and energy, and you thrill at the realization of it.

Then make the determined and unrelenting
effort to think only His thoughts and to see
and hear only the good and perfection in
everything and everyone, resolutely shutting
your eyes and mind to appearances and looking right through them to the good they hide.

You can do this—if you will. You can
find good anywhere—if you truly look for it.
For with such a desire in your heart you con-
nect up with the good—your God Consciousness—within, which will illumine your mind
and enable you to see with your Spiritual
eyes and to hear with your Spiritual ears
what is hidden from mortal consciousness.

With every loving desire to please this
God-You, you will find help given you to do
it, especially when you earnestly put your
trust in Him. When you do thus trust Him,
you will learn what He means when He says:

*"If you abide in Me, and let My Words
abide in you, you can ask what you will and
it will be done unto you."*

For when your trust becomes absolute you

will not want anything any more, for you will *know* that all He is and has is yours. And there will be no more need to ask, as He will be giving you continually of the riches of His Kingdom, whose store is inexhaustible.

This then, dear friend, is what we would have you do—to strive every moment of the day, no matter what you are doing, to abide in His Consciousness, to put all your trust in Him, leaving everything to Him, KNOWING that He will do all things through you perfectly, as you keep your mind free from doubts, fears, worries, untrue thoughts, and concern about results. For you thus enable him truly and freely to live His life in you, do His will in you, be His Self in you, even as He intended and has been preparing you for all your mortal life.

GOD AND MAMMON

In the following verses from the Sermon on the Mount is found all that anyone needs to know who is facing the tribulations now being visited upon humanity and is seeking the reason and purpose of it all and how to be free from them.

We will point out to you how wonderfully it all applies to this very question we have been discussing and how it perfectly confirms all that was stated. We will start with these significant words:

"No man can serve two masters; for either he will hate the one and love the other; or else he will cling to the one and neglect the other. You cannot serve God and mammon."

Think carefully what this means. How many of you are not trying to serve two masters? Yes, you are trying to serve God, but who of you at the present time are not fearing money and its power? Who are not bowing down before it, daily acknowledging its power over you, afraid to do anything because of the control it has over most of your thoughts and acts? In fact is not its influence such that it receives now ten times—nay, one hundred times—more of your thoughts than does God? And yet you say you are not serving mammon!

Dear friends, you cannot continue this way. You cannot any longer serve two masters. The time has come when you must decide whom you will serve — God or mammon. For why think you these tribulations are being visited upon mankind? It is because in the past you have been trying to serve both God and mammon, and now both have withdrawn their support and are letting you cast for yourself. So you are finally learning that you or yourself can do nothing, and you are now facing the necessity of choosing whom you will serve and to whom you will give all your allegiance — for when you do choose that is what will be required of you.

And this applies particularly to all seekers after Truth, but includes also those who may in any way have claimed God's help. For those who are truly serving Him, placing *all* their trust in Him, are unaffected by present conditions and are continually prospered. While those who have given full allegiance to mammon are likewise greatly prospered — seemingly; but their time of reckoning has not yet come.

We are not interested in the latter, however.
Our thoughts are for you—you who are
anxious to serve God and to free yourself
from the power of mammon forever. To you
Jesus' words are especially directed. Hear
them, for they are actual promises and contain very definite and unmistakable instructions for you:

> *"Therefore I say unto you, Be not
> anxious about your life, what you shall
> eat, or what you shall drink; nor about
> your body, what you shall wear. Is not
> the life of more value than food, and
> the body than raiment?*
>
> *"Observe the birds of the air; for they
> sow not, neither do they reap, nor
> gather into barns; yet your heavenly
> Father feeds them. Are you not of
> greater value than they?*
>
> *"Besides, which of you by being
> anxious can prolong his life one mo-
> ment? And why are you anxious about
> raiment? Consider the lilies of the field
> how they grow; they toil not neither do*

they spin; and yet I tell you, that Solomon in all his glory was not arrayed like one of these.

"Wherefore, if God so clothes the grass of the field, which today is and tomorrow is cast into the oven, shall He not much more clothe you, O ye of little faith?"

Here you are told plainly the difference between what is required of those who would serve God and those who serve mammon. The former are clearly shown that they need not be overly concerned about the affairs of their life — about food, drink and clothes; for they are promised that *God will take care of all these things — if they trust Him.* Besides they know that it is His life that is in them, even as in the birds and the lilies, and surely He will feed and clothe and provide for His own life.

But does mammon require such trust? No, he ever holds over his servants the whip of fear of loss, lack and poverty until they become abject slaves to his slightest wish.

The former in their efforts to please God

develop and portray a life of loving and self-less service. While the latter as they yield more and more to mammon develop into cold and hartless beings, thinking only of how to satisfy their utterly selfish lusts. But listen further to Jesus' words:

> *"Therefore be not anxious saying, what shall we eat or what shall we drink, or wherewithal shall we be clothed?*
> *"For all these the Gentiles seek, and your heavenly Father knows you have need of all these things.*
> *"But seek ye first the kingdom of God and His righteousness; and all these things shall be added unto you."*

The Gentiles was a term used by the Jews as synonymous with "heathen" or those who were not of the "chosen people of God," and undoubtedly Jesus used it with that meaning. In other words, the chosen of God, His servants, know Him and trust him fully for all their needs. But the Gentiles, those who are not His people, are the ones who are always

anxious about what they shall eat or drink or
how they shall be clothed.

So Jesus tells us that if we will make *first*
the seeking of the Kingdom of God — the
Divine Consciousness where love and peace
abide, putting all our trust in God and giving
all our service to Him — all the things needed
in the physical world will be richly provided.
The Emphatic Diaglot translation from the
original Greek states they will be "super-
added."

> *"Be not anxious then for the morrow,*
> *for the morrow will have its own prob-*
> *lems. Sufficient for each day are the*
> *problems thereof."*

How much more plainly can it be declared
to us that we are being lovingly watched over
and cared for, that all our needs are known
and will be supplied, and that our only
thought should be a knowing that everything
will be provided for us, even as God provides
for the birds and the lilies?

Then it all resolves itself in a matter of

trusting and abiding, and of doing the thing
that is right before us to do the very best we
know how, leaving the results, tomorrow and
all else to God. Can you bring yourself to do
this, dear friends? You must decide now. This
is the time when we must choose on which
side we will stand. Only a little while remains.
Whom then are you going to serve? Do you
require more tribulations and harder tests to
help you decide?

But remember it can no longer be a half-
hearted or a divided service. That will not be
any longer permitted. The hopelessness of
such should have been proved to you from
former efforts. You must give up *all* — all that
you have and are — and follow Him; must
make Him and the finding of His Kingdom
and the living of His life FIRST in your consciousness. It must be an every-moment-of-
the-day trusting; the thought of Him must
supersede every other thought.

That is the kind of trusting He now seeks
from you. And oh, the joy and blessedness of
those who have given themselves over wholly
to Him in such trusting!

WEALTH

WEALTH

YOU, to whom I have given an abundance of that which the world calls Riches, hearken unto this My special Message to you.

You!

Who are you, that you should be thus blessed above your brothers?

Who are you, that you should be given such a privilege, when millions of your fellows apparently have nothing?

Have you ever asked yourself that question?

Have you ever satisfactorily answered it?

Or perhaps you think YOU did it all; that you have no one to thank for these so-called blessings but yourself?

Think you this is so?

Let us see.

Did you ever wonder WHY you were born

as you were, into the particular conditions that surrounded your entrance into this life?

Did you ever wonder why you had to contend with the particular conditions that surrounded and confronted you all along your journey up through life?

Did you ever wonder why YOU came equipped with the certain tendencies, qualities and powers of mind and soul you had, while your brothers and sisters and even your parents were so entirely different or came much less fortunately equipped?

Have you arrived at any satisfactory conclusion?

No?

Then listen!

I AM responsible for all this. I did it all. I chose those conditions for you to be born into. I created every condition you met in life, and forced you through them, and through every experience of whatsoever nature. It was I who brought you to where you are today.

You, of yourself, did nothing. That personality you call yourself is merely an automaton which I move to suit My purpose.

I!

Who am I?

I, Who speak with so much assurance and authority?

Be Still, and Know.

I AM YOU, your TRUE Self;

That higher, purer, supernal part of you that arouses itself as you read, which sits back and listens and judges, and points out the truth of these words to your consciousness, and which from the beginning has guided and taught you all the Truth you know today.

Not that personality you show to the world and which you THINK is yourself; not that proud, selfish mask of a self that has been feeding you on error all these years.

For I AM your REAL Self, that Something in you which you KNOW has made you all you REALLY are, that has inspired, and cautioned, and chided, and urged, and led you on and on, despite hardships, obstacles, suffering, failure, until you have, in a dim, half-conscious way grown to rely upon It, without knowing definitely why.

Yes, I AM that Something. I AM that Divine SELF of you, abiding deep within your human personality, almost stifled by its worldly ideas, its selfish desires, its foolish pride and ambitions, yet ever seeking, longing, yearning to make you conscious of My existence, of My REAL Identity.

Yes, My child, that Something AM I, I, Who from the beginning have been sitting here within, quietly waiting for this moment. Yet while waiting it was really I Who was guiding you all the time, Who put each thought into your mind, made you do everything you did, and Who utilized the foreknown result of each thought and act so as eventually to bring you and others to a final conscious recognition of Me.

And if I have permitted you to feed on these worldly ideas, to follow these selfish desires, to grow fat with pride, and even to gain the summit of all your ambitions, it was only that you might learn the hollowness of it all, and that you could awaken to the realization that there is something else, something which the SOUL of you yearns to bring forth.

Yes, I have "blessed" you by giving you all these things you sometime in the past desired, desired so strongly that you FORCED Me to give them to you. For Desire is the agent of My Will, and supplies you with everything you want, if you want it with sufficient power to compel It to serve you.

But have these things proved the blessings you thought and expected? Have you gotten out of them real enjoyment, and is your heart now at peace?

If not, why?

It is only because you have failed to recognize Me, your True Self, as the Giver, and have used them not at all in My service, but only to satisfy your own selfish pleasure.

But I have allowed you to indulge yourself to your heart's content with all such empty joys, even leading you on from one to another, holding out to you the possibility of finding in some new bauble, or sensation, or accomplishment, or power, that something you craved, but which, alas! you have never found and never even glimpsed,—except, perhaps, when in the hours of deepest remorse and penitence you turned from this world of self you created around you to the Ideal within, and dimly sensed THERE My Presence.

Ah, dear son, I have indeed given you these blessings, and they ARE *REAL* blessings; for they are My special sign of approval to YOU.

But the blessings are not what you think them to be. The real blessings are in the qualities I have developed in you in the acquirement of these riches, in the attainment of these desires,—the qualities of determination to win, of persistency of purpose, the power to do, the ability to master every natural fault and weakness that stand in the way; all of which are but different phases of My Will, the USE of which I have been teaching you, that later on I can manifest in and through you, with your consent, My Will in Spiritual ways, even as you have been manifesting It in worldly ways.

In other words, all attaining, whether it be

of money, power or fame — in art, literature or
music, science, philosophy or religion, is
but so much training in the USE of My Will;
and therefore labor, business, science, religion, the arts or the professions, are merely
incidents, or the outer means I use to develop
in you the CONSCIOUS use of My Will.

You may think it is YOUR will that is so
acting, but so long as you consider yourself
as separate from Me, and you use this will
only to please yourself, it naturally IS self-
will, and that is why it brings you no lasting
or tangible good, only trouble, unhappiness,
and heartache, when the novelty of possession
wears off. And so, of course, you cannot
know Me, and therefore cannot acknowledge
that ALL that you do, or have, or suffer, is
but the result of the action of MY Will
working thus in and through you to bring
about My Purpose.

But the time is coming when you will
understand somewhat of this. Hence this
Message. Hence this special favor to you.

You may ask, why I, God, the Omnipotent
One, the all Good, the all Wise, made such

an unequal distribution of My Blessings, of
My Substance, of My Intelligence, of the use
of My Will, giving to the few the vast surplus,
and to the many such a pitiful lack.

You may well ask, for that is the problem I
have given you and all to solve.

But as I have enabled you partly to solve
this problem, even though you do not know
it, I will now disclose to you some of its
apparent mysteries.

II

KNOW, My son, that I give no thing to anyone unless that thing has been earned by him. By earned, I mean, grown ready for it, through desiring it so strongly that he finally draws from Me, his all-powerful, perfect SELF within, sufficient life-force and vital energy to compel conditions and circumstances to yield up and other intelligences to supply the necessary means and substance to provide form or actuality for that thing.

So it is that sometime in the past, either in this life or in a previous existence, you had arrived at the point where I could inspire in you the Idea of possessing Wealth.

I could do this, for you had grown in Soul stature and strength so that it had come time to awaken and develop in you certain of your Soul qualities and faculties which I needed for use in My service.

So I implanted in your mind the Idea of possessing Wealth or Riches. This Idea, following the usual course of Nature, in the process of time, put forth its rootlets within the soil of world conditions. These rootlets of determination, persistence, daring, doing, saving, seeing only success ahead, undiscouraged by obstacles, never recognizing failure, pushed their way unerringly to the most fertile soil, through and past all obstacles, deep into the earth nature. Likewise and at the same time a little shoot from the Idea pushed its way up towards the light and gradually began to show itself above the surface of your mental and material life. This shoot, which was the STOCK of the Idea of Wealth, grew fast, when once firmly rooted, and it soon became a sturdy, wide-spreading tree.

That tree is the outward manifestation of your life today. The nature and kind of a tree is what your character is. Its leaves are your money; its fruit just what the possession of that money has meant to you. If there is decay or unsoundness in root, trunk or branch, it is because of error, wrong or disease somewhere in the tree, which finally will destroy it unless remedied or removed.

Is there any error, wrong or disease in

YOUR tree, My son? Are there any worms gnawing their way into its heart?

Let us see. Let us search deep beneath the surface soil of world conditions, with its finely worked out system of "legitimate" methods, and its politically gained protection of the law. Let us look underneath the bark of selfishness, with its human beliefs and opinions regarding the rights of the strong. Let us peer into the cracks and crotches, the dark places in your life which are carefully hidden from the world. Let us look unflinchingly into all these places, and see if there are not some rotten spots.

Have you attained all this Wealth by absolutely honorable and righteous methods? Has any part of it been gained by sharp business practices,—yes, legitimate from the law's standpoint, but not from Mine, your True Self's? Was part of it gained by deception of friends or partners? Part by taking advantage of trusts imposed in you? Part by going through bankruptcy and settling for a percentage of your just debts? Part by riding roughshod over weaker Souls? Part by deliberate fraud? Part by any means which aroused a protesting voice within you, and which voice, in moments of quiet and solitude, ever appears to remind and accuse?

Ah, My dear child, can you truly say that none of the Wealth you possess is thus tainted?

Yes, I know, and understand.

And dear one, if you have suffered, and have regretted, and are now seeking to make restitution, it is because you have listened to My Voice, and are beginning to recognize and long for My guiding influence in your life.

But if you deny, and loudly proclaim that none of the above applies to you, and you still refuse to listen to My loving Voice within, wee, faint, almost drowned by the loud tumult now going on in your heart,—know, dear one, that you, too, must suffer, must enter into a life of heartache and misery and sorrow, into which I must plunge you, in order to purge your Soul of the pride, self-will and self-love that now control you; so that you, too, can awaken to My Love and thus learn to hear and know My Voice, ever

seeking to point out to you the true way of
Life.

As for your brothers, many, very many, I
do not yet deem ready to receive the Idea of
acquiring Wealth. In many others the Idea has
been planted, and they are merely feeling the
quickening power of Desire, My agent. Others
are forced by Desire to think and strive, and
are beginning to see the means of future
acquirement. And still others are in the act
of producing tangible results.

With all, however, I AM merely using the
Idea of Wealth, and the motive power of
Desire for its acquirement, to develop those
Soul qualities and mental faculties which will
enable Me finally and fully to bring into
manifestation their Real Self, I, God within
them, that through them My Will may be
made manifest on earth even as It is in
Heaven.

With you, My blessed one, in whom I have
brought to complete fruition My Idea of
Wealth in the form of Money and Possessions,
and who as My custodian are now capable
and ready consciously to co-operate with Me

in its use in My Service, when you can be convinced that I, God, will direct you in such use,—know that soon, very soon, you will become conscious that I AM within you, and that you need not go without to any other authority to learn this great fact. For I will cause you to KNOW that I AM leading and guiding you, and will gradually open up to your consciousness My Plan and Purpose for the Use and distribution of ALL that I have given you.

You, who have already heard My Voice within, and are seeking to satisfy Me by giving a portion of your wealth to churches, or libraries, or scientific research, or charity, or settlement work, or other enterprises, thinking My Voice can be stilled that way, and that the yearning hunger in your heart may be thus appeased:

Know that such acts are all in vain, for never can I thus be satisfied. My Voice will become only more insistent, as you strive by giving merely a portion of the wealth you hold and which is ALL Mine and none of it yours, in such effort to please Me.

For, My child, I AM already pleased with
you. Are you not what I have made you?
Is not all you have done what I permitted and
even caused you to do?

And if I have permitted you to try to
propitiate Me by using your Wealth in such
manner, it is only because such was all I
could make you understand at the time of
My Purpose surging within you.

Therefore, when, in your desire to please
Me, you attract to you many who ask you
to give of your abundance to this or that
charity, to this or that project for helping
humanity, and what you call your business
judgment tells you what is given will not be
used properly or wisely for such purposes,
and you do not respond,—know that you
have likewise been led thus to refuse by Me,
Who thus chose for you, even as I chose for
you to give to those other enterprises; and
all this for the fulfilling of My Purpose.

For I have not only reserved this Wealth
I have given you for a special Service, and
I have chosen you as My Agent in its

distribution in the way I shall disclose to you all in due season; but I AM preparing your human mind so that you can understand it is not your Wealth I want, but YOU. I want you to know that you and I are One; that I, your REAL Self, must now rule; that self-will and self-pleasure must die, and My Will and My Pleasure must live and be FIRST and ALL with you from now henceforth.

Therefore, I AM preparing your mind so that I can speak direct to your Soul consciousness from within, and I AM quickening your heart so you can become wholly conscious of My Presence therein.

So, beloved, if I say I want YOU, ALL of you; heart, soul, mind, body,—all you are, all you have, all you ever hope to be or have, I say it because I want My own,—YOU the mortal expression of My Self.

The time has come when you must know We are ONE, that there is no separation, no difference—only as you think there is. Hence, all you have or are is Mine and always has been Mine and Mine only. And now I claim My own.

My own MUST come to Me. My claim
you MUST recognize. And you MUST give
back ALL, —every penny, your home, lands,
securities, business; your body, intellect,
heart, faculties, will, your whole personality
—every loved possession, even the dearest
treasure of your heart.

For not until you have brought all and
laid them at My feet, and said, "Here, Father,
take ALL. Take and use, and only let me serve
Thee. Command and henceforth I will obey;"

Not until you thus come in true humility,
with a desire as strong to give to Me as the
one which impelled you to get for self; not
until your Soul is so possessed with a yearning
to serve Me and to rest Its wearied heart in
My Love that It can no longer be denied,—
can you ever enter into My Kingdom.

Long ago to another people I said, "It is
easier for a camel to go through a needle's
eye than for a rich man to enter the kingdom
of God."

This is just as true today. For he whom I
have deemed worthy to express the qualities
of Soul I AM now expressing through you

cannot easily humble himself,—cannot reduce that haughty personality, which so long has led and ruled, so he can go through the narrow gate of self-abnegation and self-denial.

Yet I say unto you, you must come to that, if you would enter into My Kingdom.

This is all foolishness, you say. You cannot enter the Kingdom of God here on earth. Even if you could, you would have to be shown of what practical value such an attainment was to one in business, with a family, and all the associations and responsibilities of large and varied interests.

Let us see if it is not possible to find that Kingdom and to enter it right here on earth.

III

LISTEN! And ponder.

Are you not seeking happiness, peace, health, love, the fullness of life here on earth?

Think you you will find them in the things and practices of the world? Have you not learned the futility of that?

Think you you can be truly rich and truly happy, when millions of your brothers are in poverty and misery?

No, My child; not until you have risen above all the illusions of this world of yours, have had your sight cleared by misery and suffering, have felt the poverty of love, have hungered for the TRUE Bread of Life, and have finally gotten a taste of it through forgetting self and serving your brothers, with My Righteousness as the guiding influence of your life, — can you ever find true happiness, find that peace, that harmony, that love your Soul craves. But when you HAVE found THAT, then you have indeed entered into My Kingdom.

I AM come to you now to help you find that Kingdom, to make you aware of My

Presence, I, that Something deep down in your heart that yearns for the highest, for PERFECT expression; that craves for the true riches of life, which now you know all the money in the world cannot supply.

I, God, within you, AM speaking straight from out the depths of your heart, from My Kingdom there, sweeping aside all your accumulation of worldly ideas, beliefs and opinions, and am talking direct to your Soul consciousness.

For the time is come when you must awake to your Divine mission, to the REAL purpose of your coming into this world, into this life, into this personality, into the possession of these qualities, this ability, which entitled you to be the custodian of the Wealth I have given you,—but only for such purpose.

The time is come for you to know this, to know Me, that within you which gave you this desire for wealth, which gave you the power to acquire it, which inspired and impelled and guided your every effort to attain it, and finally which now gives you the desire to use SOME of it in My Service.

Can you not see that Something is I, your own True Self, yes, God within you, the only God you will ever know, the God Who is not only dwelling and working thus in the Kingdom within you, but within your every brother, be he high or low, rich or poor, wise or ignorant; the God Who is gradually evolving your human personalities, with their mortal bodies, minds and intellects, so that He can eventually through you express ALL of His Divine qualities, even as it is in Heaven?

So I have been evolving and unfolding you so that I can find perfect expression through you, just as I evolve the Rose,—first the bud-shoot, then the bud, finally unfolding its petals,—so that through it I can show forth some of My perfect fragrance and beauty.

But you I have chosen to be a CONSCIOUS worker and expressor with Me. I have chosen you to be the means by which I AM going to bring great Joy and Happiness into this world of sorrow, discouragement, discontent and misery. I have chosen you to be the avenue

through which I AM going to pour many
Blessings into the hearts and lives of thousands of your brothers.

Would you like to work thus with Me, My
son?

Would you not like to be such an avenue,
to participate in this Joy and Happiness, to
become a partner with Me in its distribution,
—with Me, your own True Self?

Think! Think what it would mean!

Is it possible? Could you really be a partic-
ipator? you ask.

Yes, and all you need to do is to turn within to Me, with perfect Faith and Trust, and
let Me show you the way. All it needs is for
you to be CONSCIOUS of Me, abiding thus in
your heart, inspiring your every thought,
word and act, no longer listening to self-
will and self-interest, but only to Me, your
Higher Self, as I tell you of My plans and
open up to you the wonderful visions of what
I have in store for you, if you faithfully
follow My instructions.

Ah, My son, if you only would! If you
only could know the Glory that awaits

compliance with this longing surging in your
heart!

Then indeed would you be in Heaven, right
here on earth. And such Joy and Peace and
Rest would be yours, that your very Soul,
even now at the thought of it, almost bursts
its bounds in its yearning that it may be.

Then would Life be a continual song of
gladness, for the Sun of My Love would
shine continuously from out your heart,
lighting and blessing you all along the way.

Then would We joyfully start out each day
to Our business or task, be it whatever it may,
you letting Me do the leading, and you waiting upon My every Word, resting and trusting
absolutely in My Wisdom and Judgment,
KNOWING that the thing We do will always be
just the RIGHT thing, and that all that We do
will bring SUCCESS, no matter what We under-
take.

How would you like to form such a partnership, My son?

Would that not be better than spending
most of your time worrying about business or
investments, or what to do with surplus,

income, or profits, in order to get the most
returns for them; fearing continually, when
approached by friends or acquaintances, that
they are trying to interest you in some
favorite scheme, or in some unwise specula-
tion, or some craftily conceived plan to
relieve you of some of your money?

Yes, if you would but enter into partnership with Me, letting Me be the elder partner,
throwing all responsibility upon Me, then
indeed would you be relieved of all this; and
you would find, instead of cares and burdens
and problems, now so exacting they leave you
not one moment's peace of mind, that all this
has been lifted from you forever, and Life
has become one glad round of happy days,
filled to the brim with Soul-satisfying experiences, because wholly devoted to making
others happy.

IV

AND now, My son, what say you?

What are you going to do about it?

I have shown you who and what you are; that you are nothing; that I AM, and you are NOT,—you being only one of My mortal expressions, which I have brought into be-ing in order to manifest on earth through you some of My Divine qualities, and to bring Joy and Peace and Good-Will into the hearts of many of My other and less complete expressions.

I have shown you all this. And you may not believe it. But that makes no difference. You can believe or not, as you choose. But whichever you choose, know it is really I Who choose, and not you. And if you dis-believe, it is only because I AM not yet ready for you to entertain this belief; for you still have many disillusionments, disappointments, heartaches and sufferings to go through before you can come into true understanding of My meaning.

But mark you, My son! The words I herein speak are seeds I AM planting in your heart, and they will germinate, and the time will come when the Truth of them will appear plainly to your understanding.

Then you will know I AM in you, that I AM YOU, that I, your TRUE Self, must and will rule; and that all I have said herein shall blossom forth in actual manifestation in your life.

You who understand and whose heart urges you to enter into full partnership with Me; you, beloved, I here promise, shall soon partake of the Heavenly Joy that awaits.

In the meantime, your work lies before you. You must BE STILL, and learn to KNOW I AM GOD, WITHIN you. You must study and meditate on this and My other Revelations. You must realize that I, God, AM all that there is; that I gave you all, and that I can take away all.

You must accustom yourself to this Truth, and must make ready to give back all to Me for USE in My service.

But, dear son, in giving all to Me, fear not;

I, God, AM no outside person, I AM only your Real Self, your own True, Wonderful, Perfect SELF.

I ask you to give to no one but Me, your TRUE Self, and then only that I may direct and guide you in its USE. Instead of holding for self, you now will hold for Me. Instead of seeking your pleasure, you now will seek only Mine.

Henceforth you are to abide in Me and let My Words abide in you, and just to the extent you do this, you can ask what you will and it will be done unto you.

Be Still! — and KNOW — I AM — GOD.

Know that I AM holding in reserve for you wonderful uses for the Wealth I have brought into manifestation through you, uses different from any I have heretofore shown unto man. I have long been preparing you so that you can cooperate with Me in such use.

How would you like to see Man, your brothers, many of them, thousands of them, hundreds of thousands, quickened as you have been quickened with the realization of My Presence within? How would you like to

see them awakened to the consciousness of
the possession of qualities and powers similar
to those you possess, and which, with Me to
guide and direct their use, will lift them and
you to such heights your human minds now
cannot conceive?

How would you like to see the down-and-
outs, the failures, the discouraged, the dis-
contented, the weak, the sick, all awakened
to their Divine heritage, to the knowledge
that ALL that I, the FATHER, have is theirs;
and that each and all can be shown HOW to
attain it — all that WANT to know, and ASK
to be shown?

How would you like to live in a commun-
ity, in a world, where all were alike expressing
My highest qualities and powers, where each
was seeking so to eliminate his personality,
with all its limited selfish ideas, beliefs and
opinions, that My Perfect Life can express?

Would that not be a beautiful world?
Would that not be the real Heaven?

Dear son, that is what is coming into manifestation. It is coming despite all appearances
to the contrary. The realization of this Heaven

has already come to many. It is coming soon
to many more, and later to all, as My quickening Power is brought to them, even as It has
now been brought to you, and which first
must come from without before it can manifest within.

If you would like to hasten its coming, dear
son, I hereby give you that privilege. If you
would like to help make it possible that
thousands and thousands of your brothers
can come into the Great Awakening, can
come into possession of My DIVINE Qualities
and Powers, then Beloved:

Turn within to Me, and seek earnestly to
KNOW My Purpose. Pray unceasingly, until
I disclose it all, My Blessed One.

Ask and ye SHALL receive. Seek and ye
SHALL find. Knock and it SHALL be opened
unto you.

THE TEACHER

THE TEACHER

YOU, who have heard the Call of The Christ, and have consecrated yourself and your life to the service of Humanity;

You, who have felt the Divine urge to give to others of the Spiritual blessings you have received;

You, who have assumed the position of Teacher and Leader to the hungering Souls that have come to you to be fed;—

Hear this, My special Message, to you.

You, beloved, are My chosen Minister. You I have selected to be an avenue through which I shall pour many blessings into the world.

Yes, I have called you apart, and have pointed out to you the vast work there is to do, the millions of sleeping Souls waiting for the touch that will rouse them to a consciousness of the *real* purpose of their being here, in this life.

I have shown you wherein you can help
in this Work, and have proven to you that
you are truly helping, by the appreciation
and gratitude of those whom I have brought
to you and enabled you to help.

Yes, you feel you are not working in vain,
and although the way may appear dark and
uncertain and the means and ability to continue may not be in evidence, yet something
within compels you to keep on, telling you
that *all* will be taken care of in due season, —
if you prove faithful to the cause you have
made your own.

I recall all this to you, even though it may
not have appeared thus clearly before to your
mortal consciousness. I point this out in
order to prepare you for what I now have
to say.

For I now desire you to know that I have
a definite Plan and Purpose in all this, and
that the time is here when you may become
a conscious co-worker with Me in its fulfill-
ment; the point in your Spiritual Life has
been reached when your *true* place in My
Plan and an understanding of My Purpose

will be revealed to you,—if these words meet with a real response in your heart, and you strive earnestly henceforth to obey the instructions I herein shall give.

I!

Who am I?

I, who speak with so much authority, and make such all-inclusive claims?

Who am I that I can instruct *you,* and can promise rewards which only God can give?

Listen!

I AM *YOU,—*

Your own *True* SELF!

I AM your True Self, the Spirit of the Christ, Whose call you heard;

I AM your Higher Self, the Quickener, Whose urge you felt;

I AM your Divine Self, the Giver of all the Blessings you received;—

I AM, GOD, *within* you.

No, not a *separate* Spirit, dwelling somewhere within your body.

I AM *You,* your very SELF!

Yes, I, GOD, AM *YOU,* your *REAL* Self,

all of you,—body, mind, soul, consciousness, will.

I, God, your *Real* Self, speak herein these words of *living* Truth.

And the way you may *know* it is I, Who speak,—

If these words find any response within you, then it is because I, your Real Self, thus respond, and compel your attention, that you may seek to understand all of My meaning hidden herein.

But if there is no response within, and your human intellect tells you this is but another attempt to enlist your interest in some other teacher's ideas, and that you have a philosophy of your own and need no instructions from others,—it is well.

But know it is not you who thus choose, but I, your all-wise and all-loving Self, Who choose for you. For I have other ideas for you, and will bring you to an understanding of My Purpose and of your part in My Plan, all in due season,—when I have fully prepared your human mind and your *Soul* consciousness so you can receive it.

However, if you hear a Voice within, faint, scarcely intelligible, telling you to read on, and perhaps there may be something of value herein; even though you think you already know your part in My Plan and are now fulfilling My Purpose,—do not refuse. For it is My Voice trying to be heard above the tumult in your human consciousness, gently urging you to keep your mind open, to listen carefully for Words of Truth, which I here promise you will appear abundantly, beyond measure, if you truly seek to know the Word of God.

But, in order to get the full meaning of what follows, try to *imagine* that the "I" speaking herein *is* your Real Self, your Higher Self; and, even if you do not believe it as yet, assume for the time being that it *is* your Higher Self, and thus endeavor to attain the *consciousness* of it being You, talking to your mortal mind, as if to a separate personality.

If you will persist in holding this consciousness while you read, much, very much will be added unto you in the way of Spiritual blessings, and you will sing glad praises to God that this Message came into your life.

II

You, My beloved child, who are seeking
Me, but who have not yet found Me, except-
ing as an intangible something, which has
uplifted and inspired and led you on and on,
ever into narrower and yet brighter paths,
compelling you to reach out a helping hand to
every needy one you meet;

You, who are conscious of Me as the Christ
Love within your heart, and who seek to
spread the Message of His Love abroad, sow-
ing it in every heart that appears ready to
receive it;

You, to whom I have come in radiant
flashes of Light, or in visions, either sleeping
or waking, as Truth, illumining your mind
so that for the time being you see clearly the
Reality of My Spiritual Life and the illusori-
ness of all things that appeal to the outer
senses; and you are now seeking to teach
others this Truth;

You, who have become conscious of Me
as the indwelling Life within you, and it

manifests to you as Power, and enables you not only to show forth My Life in your body as vibrant Health, but it permits you to transmit this Life to others, vitalizing, strengthening and healing them, and thus bringing them to the consciousness of My Life within their bodies;

You, whom I have led a little further, whom I have taught the use of some of the laws of My Being, having quickened in you certain inner faculties and powers, which seemingly set you apart from your fellows, so that you now call yourself an occultist, and are seeking to attain the complete mastery of these powers of self;

Yes, and even you, My blessed one, who are conscious of Me as your Divine Self, as God within you, and who are drawing from Me freely My Love, My Wisdom, and My Power, and who are teaching this Great Truth and attracting to you many followers who hail you as an Illumined One;—

To you, one and all, I bring this, My Message of the *Impersonal Life.*

The idea of the "Impersonal" may not be

new to you. You may have pondered over it.
You may have striven more or less to live it.
You may even have taught it to your
followers, and yet you may have no comprehension of its real meaning.

It is My Purpose now to make you conscious of that meaning, so that you as Teacher
and Leader to others no more can have the
excuse of not knowing it, when I hereafter,
from within, insist that My *Impersonal Life*
shall manifest in and through you. For I,
your True Self, henceforth will be satisfied
with nothing less.

So follow carefully all I now shall say,
and seek earnestly to know My *real* meaning,
— its personal and vital application to you,—
before passing it by or discarding it, should
that impulse come to you.

I AM first going to ask some questions.

In asking these questions, I AM directing
them straight to your *Soul* consciousness.
Necessarily they will have to go through
your mortal mind. As your mortal mind is
but a part of your mortal self or your human
personality, it first becomes necessary that

you learn the ways of the mortal mind and see this self as it really is — not as you fancy it is, — see this personality of yours pretend to feel hurt, commence to rebel and deny, and even to grow indignant, if not angry, at these questions. For I AM going to probe to the quick, right to the center of its self-complacency, its self-righteousness, its spiritual pride, its love of power, of leadership, of being thought very wise and good,—if any of these qualities still exist in your personality.

But remember, it is not *you* who are feeling hurt, or who rebel or grow angry. It is only your personality. For *you* are really I, your own True Self, and I AM asking these questions, and I AM showing up to you these qualities, insisting that *all* that stands in the way of My Perfect *Impersonal Life* expression henceforth can have no place in your life.

If you watch carefully and study the thoughts and feelings that come to your mind as you read the questions, you will, perhaps, discover a phase of your nature you thought was no longer in evidence. But the special mission of this Message is to make you fully aware of such phase, and of all phases of your human nature, that have not yet come under My, your True Self's, dominion.

This is *inner* teaching, and it is an *inner* work which you will now be called upon to do, with Me, your own Higher Self, as Teacher.

If your Soul responds, and you fearlessly are willing to accept anything I have to say, and will accept it in true humility and understanding of Spirit, know that great Spiritual Joy awaits you and many Blessings will follow.

But if your personality still insists that the "I" speaking herein is merely some person, who considers him or herself divinely ordained, and who is taking an unwarranted liberty in thus obtruding into your private affairs; and that you need not answer the questions even to yourself, for they are no one's business but your own; if your personality, with its merely human mind, so persuades you,—it is well, and I needs must teach you in some other and much harder way.

Yet it is all true; these questions *are* no one else's business. They are only *your* business. But remember, I, your own True Self, God within you, alone AM asking them. And I AM asking them only that you may *face your self,* that you may see clearly this personality of yours, with all its human weaknesses, faults and misconceptions that still exist, and which, through your inability to perceive their subtle influence over you, are hindering the perfect expression of My Impersonal Life in and through you.

And if I shall prick the bubbles of all such illusions of the personality still lurking around in your mental atmosphere, after first showing up clearly their unreality, it is only in order that, should they again appear, you will immediately recognize them and refuse them entrance into your life.

Perhaps your personality is saying, as you read, that none of this applies to you, that you need no such instructions.

Think you so? Then answer to Me, your

True Self, the following questions, carefully studying your *feelings,* after reading each, with soul-searching analysis:—

Are you sure, My child, there is nothing of self, seeking for self, in this work you claim to be doing for Humanity?

Are you sure you, personally, are not taking the credit for the help your students and followers are getting through you?

Are you quite sure you are not feeling a secret pleasure and pride in their attitude of admiring respect and awe towards you?

These teachings you are giving out,—are you certain they are direct from Me, your Divine Self? Or are they but your personal views, the thoughts you have gathered from other human teachers?

Are you tainting this Work I have given you to do by subtly introducing your personality into it, drawing attention more to you as teacher, than turning them to Me within themselves, their only *true* Teacher?

Can you truly say you have only loving and helpful thoughts, and speak only The Christ's words, when asked or when talking about other teachers and leaders, no matter who they be?

When meeting with other teachers and leaders, do you never push your self forward, never desire to lead or impress them with your personality or your powers?

When you meet one who has come into a higher realization of God than you, does only the purest, brotherly love go out from you to that Soul?

When one of your own pupils, through your aid, awakens to the presence of Me within, and quickly attains to an even greater consciousness of My Powers than have you, do you sincerely rejoice with great rejoicing, and praise God for His Blessings to that one?

Are you sure, beloved, you are doing all that you do without thought of reward, caring naught for results, resting only in the consciousness that I AM doing it all, and that I AM responsible?

Do you truly realize that you and your personality are one, that there is no difference; and do you fully understand your own self, and *know* your identity with Me, God, your Divine Self?

In all your teachings of these high Truths, do you, *in your Soul,* recognize the oneness of All; that I, God, am All there is; that All there is *you are;* that I AM your Real Self; that there is no separation; that *all that you do God does;* that you are One with God, and all God's powers are your powers?

Are you sure, My child, that all the things you are teaching you, yourself, *ARE;* that you are doing, manifesting, LIVING *all* that you preach to others?

If you can truly answer satisfactorily to Me, your Higher Self, all these questions, then this Message is not for you, and you need read no further; for you know already all that I AM going to say.

But if you are *not* sure, and realize that your personality is still a more or less dominating factor in your life, then it would be wise to read on. For I AM now coming to the vital part of My Message.

III

Ah, My beloved, how shall I tell you? How can I penetrate through the wall of unconscious self-righteousness, of self-sufficiency, of spiritual pride and independence, which your personality has built up around you, perhaps, and which often prevents My Words of Truth, spoken through others, reaching your Soul consciousness?

How can I get past the feeling which even now, maybe, is flooding your human consciousness, rousing your ire and opposition, so that you may not grasp the deep significance of My meaning?

Can you not see, if such feeling is manifesting in your heart, that your personality is still much in evidence — when it can so control you? Can you not understand that, not until words such as the above, coming from any source whatsoever, can create in you nothing but a sympathetic comprehension of their loving and helpful intent; and that, should any feelings of a rebellious or antagonistic nature arise, not until you can immediately recognize them and their source, and can proceed to transmute them into love and gratitude to Me for thus pointing out to you these weaknesses that still exist, — can you be a pure and true channel through which the Christ teachings can flow?

Can you not see that when one sets one's self up as a teacher to others, and assumes to act as a mediator between them and God, and to interpret for them His Will and His Meaning, that one takes upon one's self a great responsibility, — unless one is resting wholly in the consciousness of God and His Love, so that God is able to speak and act through one's human mind and body without let or hindrance of any kind?

And it is to enable the sincere and true seeker after God, him who would earnestly strive to abide in Him and to let His consciousness abide in his heart, if he but knew how; him who yearns only to know His Will, that he may obey It and serve Him in every possible way, — it is to enable such to know I, the True Self within, *AM God,* beyond peradventure of a doubt, that these words are written.

There are many professing to know Me, to be followers of Me, to be giving out My teachings, and who are teaching and preaching the way of at-one-ment; but, who, outwardly to others, and in their innermost thoughts, are so mixed up with their personalities, are so influenced and controlled by them, that they do *not* know Me, even though they proclaim daily that I am leading them and speaking through them. It is for such, also, that these Words are intended.

It is true I do speak through such; but not as they understand. For they, personally, even through priding themselves over the beautiful thoughts that flow from their mouths at times, and the help these thoughts are to others, know not when I speak and when their personality. For if they did truly know Me, they would have no pride, would take no credit to or thought of themselves; but would humbly abide in the consciousness of Me doing it all, and would let Me and My Impersonal Love rule in every detail of their lives.

Yet I speak through such proud personalities, and even through hypocrites and teachers of false doctrines, using every avenue to bring to the seeking Soul the phases of Truth needed to lead it into conscious oneness with Me. For remember, Truth is not always sugar-coated, and ofttimes it is needful that one taste of the bitter in order to appreciate the sweet and the pure.

Know you not it is through your sins, your mistakes, through deception, false friends, *wrong teaching,* that you learn and grow strong? Thus principally do I teach. I lead you through all these, that you may learn to distinguish the true from the false, the realities of life from the fallacies and illusions. The suffering and pain such learning entails is only the fire of My Love in your heart burning away the lusts of the flesh, the error thoughts, the selfishness, pride and egotism, emplanted and fostered therein by the personality, which must be removed that My Impersonal Life can freely and fully manifest.

And this personality, what is it? It is that which you, with your human mind, *imagine* yourself to be. It is the creature to which you gave birth many, many ages ago, which you have nurtured and fed, loved and fought for, trusted and followed and believed in, just as if it were real, all these years; the child of your bosom, the creature of your human mind, thought-born, when you fell away in consciousness from Me in Eden after your first sin, and ever since have fed with and bred on the idea that you were separate from Me, and that I, God, was displeased with you and have been continually punishing you for eating the fruit of the knowledge of Good and Evil.

And if I have permitted you to love and trust, follow and obey this imaginary child, now grown in your consciousness to full maturity, and become so strong and powerful that it dominates and rules its parent with a rod of iron, it is only in order that, through the sins and errors into which it drove you and the consequent suffering these brought, I might awaken you to the reality of its *unreality,* to the fact that it has no existence except in your mind; that

the only life it has and all its power, come
from your constant thinking that *you* are
this personality and are separate and apart
from Me.

And if there has awakened in you a dim
sense of its unreality, and you are now turning
within to Me, seeking to be released from the
thralldom of its rule, know that it can never
be until you are fully conscious that you and
I, God within you, are One; that there is no
separation; that all I Am you Are; that all
I have is yours; that all power is given you in
heaven and earth; and hence that I Am and
you *must be* Master, and that this personality
of yours is merely a phase of mortal thought
I permitted to be born in your human consciousness, in order to develop your mind
and body until they become strong enough
consciously to contain and fully express
My Impersonal Life.

You must be Master, absolute Master of
yourself. But you cannot be Master until
you *know* yourself, know every phase of
your personality; all your strength and all
your weakness; all your powers, physical,

mental and spiritual; all your human faults,
tendencies and limitations; and can see
yourself and know your personality even
as others see and know you, with both the
eyes and judgment of the world and the
vision and understanding of the Spirit; know
all about that personality which has so subtly
and craftily impinged itself upon your consciousness, that now you can scarcely tell
when *it* is manifesting, and when I, your
True Self.

So this personality of yours must be sub-
dued, must be merged into My Impersonality, before My true Teachings can come
forth. You must realize with Soul realization
that you, the Impersonal you, the True
you, are one with your brother, even as
you are one with Me, you must learn to see
Me, *his* Impersonal self, underneath the
illusions of *his* personality, must permit
no reflection of your own personality to
cloud the clear sight of Me therein, yearn-
ingly waiting for the time when he, too,
perhaps through you, may be led to recognize
Me abiding within *his* heart.

In the Impersonal *all* is one. When you can enter into the oneness of the Impersonal consciousness and can abide there at will, you have entered into My Kingdom and have found God; and thereafter will be able to see and know Him in all His creations. For the impersonal Consciousness is My Consciousness: It is My Kingdom, the realm of My Being; and as I AM the Life of all things, once having entered this realm you become one with Me, and therefore one with all beings; and you can go in and out and find pasture. For I will feed you with the Bread of the Spirit, and the Wine of Life will flow through you in rivers of Living Love, blessing you in all ways and likewise all whom you contact.

IV

So I tell you these things, My child, My chosen one, that you may strive unceasingly to know this personality, know all its subtly selfish phases, many of them hidden so deep within your consciousness that you are not even aware they are there. Because *you* hid them there long ages ago, having been deceived into believing them good and necessary to your life; and therefore made them part of your nature. But now, with My help, you are going to hunt them all out and cast them forth, that My Impersonal Nature can freely manifest.

As I have chosen you, My child, and have called you aside, and have permitted you to think you have a special work to do, I want you to be absolutely sure, beloved, it is *My* Voice you have been listening to while doing this work, and not the voice of your personality. If I AM to be your Teacher, and you wish *Me* to lead and direct you in this work, and you truly desire to serve Me, then must every attribute of your human personality yield itself to Me, and *you* must compel it so to do. So long as one selfish desire or instinct remains, it is sure to taint your work, and you still be under the domination of the personality.

There are many, many ways it will seek to manifest; but I AM here, and I will point out each clearly,—if you ask Me. I will tell you, not with dominating, insistent authority, nor with anxious clamorings within, but with gentle, loving suggestion, that you cannot fail to understand,—if you will but be on the alert and will listen for My Voice, which is ever counselling and directing those who wait upon Me in living faith and trust.

My work, you will gradually learn, can only be done with the spirit of *Impersonal* love in your heart. Only through such spirit— selfless, disinterested, never caring about results—can I express through you. You must yield *all* to Me, must let *Me* rule, and must leave *all* consequences to Me.

When you have learned to do that, then

will I cause to quicken in you a consciousness of your identity with Me, of My Power and My Wisdom and My Love within. Then will your personal life gradually merge into My Impersonal Life, and you will be conscious of all your Divine Heritage and of the *real* Work I have chosen for you to do.

But until your human consciousness has become merged with My Divine Consciousness, until you can truly know and *use* your Divine powers, it might be better to so live that you assume to possess no powers or wisdom above your fellows. It might be better first to prove *to yourself* that you are able to *live* and to *be* all these things you now more or less clearly see with the inner eye, before you give them out to others as Truth or as coming from God.

For you know it is only the personality that sets itself up as one of authority, or as being wise in the Spirit, as one chosen of God, and as being His mouthpiece. And remember, I AM in your students and followers, even as I AM in you. Often, very often the beautiful thoughts that come from teachers do not carry the conviction of Truth, because I cause their hearers to see only too plainly that such teachers *are not living* what they teach; or that their personalities are too dominating; or they are too desirous of giving the impression of possessing wisdom, or spirituality, or powers; or that they are unmistakably leading followers on only in order to get from them what money they can, deceiving themselves the while into believing such fallacious reasoning as "the servant is worthy of his hire," or that "in giving out spiritual teachings one must receive back material pay," that being the law.

Ah, My beloved, are you sure none of these things are noticed by your pupils or hearers in *you?* Are you sure that the money question is not occupying the most prominent place in *your* mind, and the desire to serve Me is receiving but secondary consideration? Can you truly say that you put all material problems wholly up to Me, *knowing* that I will always provide bounteously; that there is no fear in your heart, no doubts or questionings as to My always supplying every need, yea, every desire?

If so, then is it necessary to *charge* or accept *pay* for the loving help I give out through you? Is not *My* servant worthy of his hire, and will *I* not provide? Consider the lilies of the field and the fowl of the air. Who clothes and feeds them? Are you not more to Me than they? Oh, you of little faith!

Listen! Only as you give out of the fullness of Love, freely, unthinking as to reward or returns, can you receive of *My* Bounty.

But you may not accept this now. If so, it is well. For I have chosen that it be so, and that you learn the Truth through other channels. You must still hold to the belief that even God's servants must live, and that in living and working on the world plane they are compelled to use the world's methods, even in Spiritual work.

And this is true, but not as you understand it. The time will come, however, when you have learned through trial and suffering to know *My* Way, when you are able to see with My Impersonal eyes and to know with My Impersonal understanding, and can put aside altogether all personal interest in your teaching, and in both the results of and the reward for such teaching—that you will *know* how to use the world's tools even in Spiritual work.

But before that can be I may have to lead you by the *hard* way up the high mountain of Spiritual attainment,—by the *hard* way of bitter experience.

Yes, you can get there that way. But, oh, how long and heart-breaking the journey!

Perhaps, you say,—that is the only way one can learn.

No, it is only *one* way you can learn—the *hard* way. It is the personal way, and it may be necessary for some to go that way. But I seek to save you from that way.

Have you not seen the sad misfortune of some of those I have thus led up into the high mountain, those who have climbed up the hard way,—*and have fallen,* even from near the summit?

Yes, no one can rise so high but what he can fall; for the personality is always in evidence on that journey. It is the adversary who is opposing every step. That is what makes it so hard. So long as there is left anything of self, just so long will the personality find a way to oppose. I may lead you to the mountain top, and show you all the kingdoms of the air, of the earth, of fire and of water, and present them to you and tell you they are all yours to *use*. But if you have not thoroughly purged your heart, mind and Soul of self, behold! the personality appears and speaks from behind you, and so subtly imitates My Voice that you may think it is I. And when it tells you to take and use these kingdoms to glorify self, that having climbed to this great height, such is your reward,—you may trust it, and obey; yes, even as they who fell from their former high estate, into deep, outer darkness.

In order that you may be saved that journey and that temptation, My beloved, I here hold out to you the far easier and simpler way:—

If you will but abide in the consciousness of Me, the True Self within you, and let My

Holy Impersonal Love abide in you, and will permit It to flow forth freely, unhindered, unconditioned, from your heart to bless all whom you meet,—if you will but do this, you may ask of Me *whatever you will,* and it shall be done for you.

For do you not see, beloved, if you can fully harmonize your life with My Life, by eliminating all phases of the selfish personality, if you will but get out of the way with your *personal* ideas, beliefs and opinions, so that *My* Life, which is but *My LIVING Love,* can freely and fully express forth through you,—that the void left after the personal life is gone will be immediately filled—even as air rushes into a vacuum—with My Impersonal Life? For My Impersonal Life is the *real* substance of all things, and is ever seeking to express outwardly Its true nature; and all of It that is necessary to fill out and complete My Divine Nature in *you* will surely flow both into you and through you,—whenever you let It; and will harmonize and bless you and bring into outer tangible manifestation all good things needed to completely round out your human nature, and make for Joy, Happiness, Satisfaction, and Peace within your Soul.

V

And shall I now tell you about My Impersonal Life, how you may *consciously* live it with Me, and be wholly One with Me, Your True Self, your Father-in-Heaven?

Then listen! And meditate long and earnestly on all I now shall say. Do not pass by a single sentence or any one thought in it until My meaning becomes clear.

I seek nothing but to *BE* and *EXPRESS* My Self in and through you. *My Self* is purely Impersonal, for It is the Real self of every human being. I AM the pure, perfect, selfless, *inner* nature of every human self, ensouled in their physical bodies, in order to develop them into mediums for the expression of My Divine attributes on earth, even as it is in Heaven.

Therefore, you, too, must seek nothing but to *be* and express *your* True Self, which is I, your Divine, *Impersonal* Self. Thereby do you unite your purpose with Mine, your will with My Will, your nature with My Nature; and thus become One with Me, and We become Two-in-One, the Divine estate on earth.

In order that this may Be, we must purge first your heart, then your mind, and then your body, of every sense and inclination of the personal self. That can only be accomplished by My Holy *Impersonal* Love, with which I will fill your heart, so that there will be no room in it for any part of self. With the heart purified and sweetened, the mind will attract and think only pure and sweet thoughts, My thoughts, which are always pure Wisdom. Therefore you will see only Purity and Goodness in all things. Naturally, then, being no more controlled or influenced by wrong thoughts, your body will become subservient to My Life, whose vitalizing, purifying and perfecting power will drive from it all inharmonies. Then, with only My Love in your heart, My Thoughts in your mind, and My Life in your body, you will *know* I AM, your own True Self,—for then there will be no other self.

Then I AM, your True Self, will go forth
in the world, but not be *of* it. You will no
longer be attracted to or by it. But you
will see with My eyes, hear with My ears,
and know with My understanding all things.
You no longer will see only the outward
appearance of things, but you will see them in
their *Reality.* Nothing past, present or future,
will be hidden from you; for the limitations
of the human nature are no longer there, and
in the Spirit there is no time, space, personalities or separation,—*All* is *one.*

And you will go forth with the consciousness of this great Impersonal Love within
you as the very substance of your nature,
and through It I will uplift, strengthen, help
and bless all whom I will lead you to or
attract to you. Love being your *nature* and
on the earth plane in man It being the pure
and perfect *expression* of My *Life,* It is
always pushing forth in and through him
towards full, complete, harmonious outer
manifestation.

And with the consciousness of your
Divinity and of the Divine *Power* My Love

gives you, instead of parading such or giving evidence of such in any personal way, you will only give and help and bless Impersonally, seeking to remove all fetters, all hindrances, all limitations that prevent My Life in any way from expressing in and through your fellow beings.

Thus you become One with the One Life, with My Inner, Impersonal Life; therefore, One with Me, the Fount and Source of all blessings, earthly and Divine.

And therefore you will no longer *seek* to teach or lead others, because you have become *Impersonal* and being Impersonal you will let Me, *within both them and you,* do all the teaching and directing. You will no longer seek to lead, but only to *follow* Me.

And you will no longer even seek to be wise, or good, or strong, or rich, or healthy, or happy, because you *are* all these things, being One with Me, Who AM the inner essence of which these things are but the outer manifestation.

And you will *know* that all inharmony

presages the coming harmony; that all lack is but My urge towards complete expression; that all darkness is but shadow indicating the direction of the Light; that all weakness is part of the effects of training which will result in a perfected will; and that all evil is good and necessary, – to one who has attained to My Impersonal consciousness and view-point.

And so you will go about your business, whatever it be, for then you will know that *all* business is My business; and instead of seeking and striving to gain for self the Spiritual blessings that lie at the mountain top, you will cease all seeking and striving, and will have *forgotten* self; and will feel only the urge to give, and give, and give, of the Great Love within, letting *It* quicken and awaken and help and strengthen the struggling souls about you, seeking to comprehend and obey the feeling of Me within their hearts, but who, owing to their immature and untrained minds, are misunderstanding that feeling and consequently My meaning, as I try to make it known from *within*.

And I will lead them to you or you to them, that I may teach them first from *without* through you. Just as I have brought to you My Message through these words, so will I give My Message to many hundreds of others through words I shall speak through *you*. But this can not be as I purpose it, until I can live My Impersonal Life in you, until you have yielded up your human personality to My Divine Impersonality. Not until *you* determine with all the power of your will, and yearn with all the hunger of your Soul, to *live* the Impersonal Life, to make your personal self wait upon and serve Me, your own, True, Impersonal Self, can I give you even a glimpse of My Real Meaning. But when I have vouchsafed you that glimpse, My beloved, ever afterward will the glory of it be with you, and it will lead you on and on, and ever on, until My full meaning is forced from Me by the might of your Soul's Desire.

That is my Message. Its mission is to awaken in you this Desire, the Desire to live the Impersonal Life.

This is high teaching, and is only for those who can see it, for those whom I have prepared and made ready for its reception.

To such, however, it is but the door, which opens to far higher teachings, that I will give to them direct from out their own Souls,— those who come to Me in loving faith and trust, and who are willing to empty their hearts of self, that I may fill them with My Holy Impersonal Love.

For I here promise you,—I have in store for those who yearn to come to Me by the simple, loving, Impersonal way, great wonders of Spiritual Blessings, which will be to them a source of endless Joy; and that I will give to them, as I abide in them and they in Me, the *unlimited use of ALL* of My Divine Powers and Attributes.